LIFE
INSURANCE

The Secure Retirement Method

LIFE INSURANCE

The Essential Financial Tool
Everyone Loves to Hate

How to use life insurance before retirement
and in retirement to protect your family,
secure your legacy, and create your own
Secure Retirement plan.

John H. Curry

JOHNHCURRY.COM

John H. Curry
John_Curry@NorthFloridaFinancial.com

The Secure Retirement Method Life Insurance: The Essential Financial Tool Everyone Loves to Hate/ John H. Curry. —1st ed.

ISBN 978-0-9908714-3-9

CONTENTS

10/29/2021

John,

I hope you enjoy my book.

Best Wishes,

John

How will your retirement measure up?

"People come to me and my team for help in identifying the financial threats to their income and assets. We then co-create a plan to help them eliminate or reduce those financial threats."

John Curry's Secure Retirement Method

The Vision Session
You begin exploring your current situation and new possibilities for your future.

The Discovery Session
A detailed assessment and analysis of your current financial situation and a baseline to build on.

The Strategy Session
A step- by-step planning process to develop strategies, choose tools, and build a team to achieve your goals.

The Implementation Session
A system of tools, resources, capabilities, and expertise for effectively implementing you plans.

John Curry's Secure Retirement Method

Your Retirement Vision

1. Think ahead to the day of your retirement. Looking back from that day what has to have happened along the way for you to feel happy about retirement?

2. What obstacles and concerns stand in your way to achieving your vision of retirement?

3. What are the most important actions you must take to overcome these obstacles and concerns?

4. What progress have you already made toward achieving your retirement vision?

Exclusively for FRS Members

The Secure Retirement Scorecard

Name: _____ Date: _____ Phone: _____

Decide your rating on a scale of 1 (completely disagree with statement) to 10 (completely agree with statement).

	Statement	Rating										Comments
1	I understand the four options under the FRS Pension Plan.	1	2	3	4	5	6	7	8	9	10	
2	I understand my Social Security choices.	1	2	3	4	5	6	7	8	9	10	
3	I understand the Deferred Compensation Program.	1	2	3	4	5	6	7	8	9	10	
4	I understand the DROP Program.	1	2	3	4	5	6	7	8	9	10	
5	I have a step-by-step action plan to achieve my retirement goals.	1	2	3	4	5	6	7	8	9	10	
6	My finances are organized and efficient.	1	2	3	4	5	6	7	8	9	10	
7	I am confident about the performance of my investments.	1	2	3	4	5	6	7	8	9	10	
8	I have a trusted team of advisors helping me achieve my goals.	1	2	3	4	5	6	7	8	9	10	
9	I have a plan to protect and enhance my lifestyle.	1	2	3	4	5	6	7	8	9	10	
10	I have a strong sense of confidence about my future.	1	2	3	4	5	6	7	8	9	10	
Add Column Totals												**Your Score:**

If you would like to discuss your Scorecard, call 850-562-3000 to schedule a phone appointment or email John_Curry@GLIC.com.

Introduction

Life insurance is a very complicated, confusing topic.

That's why in this book, all you're going to get is straight talk. No hard-to-follow charts or graphs. Just an open conversation about the role of life insurance in your financial and retirement planning.

There are many, many—often surprising—ways you can use life insurance as a tool to benefit not just your family when you die… but also yourself and others while you're still living.

In this book, I will share those strategies. Along the way, I'm going to tell you about how life insurance has helped me personally as well as family members, friends, and, of course, clients over the years. You'll also discover that life insurance is essential for everyone, of all ages and stages in life—even young children.

Whether you have a lot of assets or not many, a high-paying job or one that's more average. No matter what walk of life you come from, life insurance can be valuable as you'll find out.

Let's start.

The Fear of Death

A friend of mine made a comment one time that normal, happy, well-adjusted people don't want to sit around talking about dying or becoming disabled. We tend to want to avoid those sorts of conversations.

By extension, life insurance can be a tough topic to talk about. But it's the talk you must have with your spouse... your family. I hope to educate you enough to dispel the misinformation about this financial tool and give you confidence to know what type will benefit you—not to mention give you comfort and confidence to speak about this difficult subject.

I'll admit, none of us really *needs* life insurance. You choose to have it... because it's the right thing to do. I heard it said early in my career that people buy life insurance because either you owe someone or you love someone.

Owe someone—that's any debt you might leave behind. Love someone... you don't want your family to just get by when you pass away. You want them to have a good future based on what you would have provided had you lived longer.

That is why I'm <u>not</u> going to pressure you to buy life insurance.

The Big Questions About Life Insurance

In this book, I'll share what I know, you take it in, and then you make the decision. You'll be able to make an educated decision whether to pursue coverage or not because we'll be covering all the key questions about life insurance you need answered:

<u>How much</u> life insurance should I buy?

What type of life insurance should I buy?
When should I buy life insurance?
Who should I buy life insurance from?

We'll also explore why life insurance can be an indispensable financial tool when you provide coverage for kids and grandkids or you're young, single, part of a young couple, have a family, are soon-to-be-retired, or retired (in fact, it can be a safer and more flexible retirement savings tool than an IRA or 401(k))... or even a business owner. And not only can life insurance be used in retirement, but you can use it any time in your life—while still alive.

I will tell you that now more than ever people should have life insurance—I'm one of those people. That's why I work in this industry.

What I've done in this book is taken the things that I've learned—the good, the bad, and the ugly over my 46 years in this industry—and I've discovered what works and what doesn't. With the information in this book, you can benefit from these lessons if you desire to.

Simply put, I want to help people benefit from life insurance if it's appropriate for them and their specific situation. What's at risk is very simple:

If you find a strategy in this book that works in your situation—and you don't take action—somebody will suffer.

Of the folks who had the foresight to do their financial planning properly and included the right type and amount of life insurance before they passed away… their families are doing better.

You can do the same when you read this book and take its lessons to heart. By the end, you will understand:

- The different types of life insurance plans—and which one you should buy.
- How much insurance you should own.
- When you should buy this coverage.
- Who you should buy it from.

The reason I'm on my soapbox about this is that I'm 68 years old. I've been in business since 1975. At the time of writing, that's 46 years of experience. When I started in financial services, all I did was sell life insurance. And I got bored with that. I wanted to do more. I wanted to do the planning side, and I was a bit of a maverick in the sense that most people in the industry stayed in their lane.

I wanted to become licensed to be able to do investment work, annuities, whatever the client needs, health insurance, disability insurance, etc. So, that was my progression over the years in being able to help clients create comprehensive financial and retirement plans.

Life insurance has always been a part of that process.

But I've discovered that because of the COVID-19 pandemic, life insurance is more important than ever. A lot of people have gotten sick; a lot of people have died. This has spurred renewed interest in making sure that a person is properly insured for their families.

The pandemic isn't the only source of urgency.

The problem is that as we get older, we have health issues. And that means we don't qualify for many types of insurance. Or, if we do qualify, the coverage is expensive. That's why it's so important to understand your options early and take action. Your decision whether or not to secure coverage can have huge ramifications for you and your family.

> *"Your decision whether or not to secure coverage can have huge ramifications for you and your family."*

Who This Book Is For

This book is for those who don't currently have life insurance but also those who have had insurance for many years but don't know if they have enough or the right type… or how they can use it beyond the death benefit.

I consider it my job to help educate people and show them how to use insurance in a way that will help them financially while still living and help their families upon death. I'm not trying to scare or intimidate anybody.

When buying a policy, you must also coordinate it in a manner that is affordable and makes sense in your personal situation.

The truth is that life insurance can be used in all different stages of life. It's a tool.

It can be used by young families, or as you near retirement, as you're in retirement, or if you're a business owner.

Hopefully, this book opens your eyes to the many ways life insurance can be used to benefit your life and that of your loved ones.

I can guarantee you will learn something that will help you change the way you're using your life insurance now. Maybe it unlocks an idea, so that you can use it in a way that you weren't aware of. Somewhere in here, you're going to find an idea that's going to be very valuable to you.

I don't care who you are or how old you are… there's a place for life insurance.

Planning, Not Products

There's a lot of misunderstanding about life insurance among everyday people. In fact, you have a lot of insurance salespeople who don't know much about life insurance. How does that happen? They've been told to go out and sell a product.

I did that too when I was 22. Back then, I only had two products: term and whole life insurance. But then, as I got serious about the planning side, I stopped trying to sell products. I started to sit down with people and have conversations about how to plan for an ideal life now and in retirement. That's what I still do today.

We talk about your goals, your dreams, your fears. What dangers and obstacles do you face? What are the opportunities out there? The idea is to talk in terms of what life looks like.

Then we find the right retirement accounts, tax strategies, investments, and, yes, life insurance, to fit that plan.

CHAPTER 1

Your Most Valuable Asset - Your Human Life Value

I F YOU'RE READING this from home, you're sitting in what you probably consider your most valuable asset: your home. From a pure asset calculation on a balance sheet, your banker would agree with you.

I say hogwash!

The most valuable asset you have is the face you see when you look into a mirror. You are your most valuable asset. It's tied to your ability to go out there and earn a paycheck, to build a business, or otherwise create an income stream.

It's called your economic value, or Human Life Value. More on this key concept in just a moment.

I think it's funny we go out of our way to make sure that our cars are fully insured and our home is insured for full replacement value. Yet, many people scrimp on life insurance, which is protecting our most valuable asset.

"We go out of our way to make sure that our cars are fully insured and our home is insured for full replacement value. Yet, many people scrimp on life insurance."

I was guilty of this misconception too until I got a proper education on this concept. Most insurance agents, whether in property and casualty or life insurance, are taught to just sell you a policy.

In the early days of my career, I did the same thing. I was told to go sell this term insurance policy… or go sell this whole life policy. And then when you get a little bit of maturity and some experience under your belt, because somebody died, for instance, and you didn't deliver enough money to their survivors… it kind of changes your mindset. It certainly changed mine.

Determining Your Human Life Value

If you don't find anything else valuable in the book, you must know this fact.

As I stated previously, when I ask most people what their most valuable asset is, they usually answer that it's their house.

But it's not. It's *your* economic value. Let me explain…

Back in 1924, Dr. Solomon Huebner promoted the concept that the proper way to determine how much life insurance you need is something called Human Life Value.

Think of it this way. You buy a house; you buy a car—those are property values. But all property values are the result of someone's Human Life Value, sometimes called economic value. They had to go out there and produce that value by earning an income.

That means you can't treat life insurance as you would other types of insurance.

Consider this: How would you insure a house that is worth $300,000? Would you settle for $100,000 in coverage in case it burns down or blows away? Do you think you could get by on that amount to rebuild that same home?

No!

It would not allow you to replace the home. It would not cover anywhere near the replacement value.

Looking at scenarios like that inspired Dr. Huebner to come up with his concept of Human Life Value… In short, every person has value. And that should be the basis of their life insurance coverage. Let's use some simple numbers to explain how.

A Case Study in Economic Value

Let's suppose someone is 35 years old. They're making $100,000 a year, and they never get a pay raise. And they retire at 65. So, that's 30 years at $100,000. Three million dollars in all. So, we could say that's their economic value.

However, they would get pay increases along the way. In wrongful death lawsuits, this is what the attorneys have to prove is financial loss—your ability to create economic value changes.

Think about it. When we first start out in life, it might appear that we don't have much value.

But if someone was killed in a wrongful death situation at 20 years old, the attorney would paint a picture to the court of a person killed in their prime who was poised to make a lot of money in their career. They would make the case for a multi-million-dollar settlement.

To determine the full economic value, we do have to factor in future pay raises. That gives you the full measure of economic value.

It makes sense, right? The point of life insurance is to replace someone's income that they would produce in the rest of their life. It can be vital for the well-being of spouses and families. Yet, many people still don't get it, and most people don't look at their economic value in this way.

They will insure cars, houses, boats…for full replacement value. But they hesitate when it comes to life insurance.

The most valuable asset they have is not their home, it's their economic value, their ability to produce an income. And that income can be lost, it can be permanently lost, because you die, or there can be a temporary loss because you became disabled, and you're out of work for a short period of time. That's why disability income insurance is so important during your working years.

The Two Philosophies of Life Insurance

One method to understand Human Life Value is by looking at the two ways to ensure your life:

The Needs Basis

For example, you have a $300,000 mortgage on your house. You are told by other so-called financial experts that when you die, you should at least make sure your debts are covered. So, when you die, the house is paid for and your spouse doesn't have to worry about it.

For some people, it stops there. No judgement on my part—although as you'll see throughout this book, it's my philosophy to have as much coverage as you can get.

My recommended approach is to get as much life insurance as possible to insure your full economic or human life value and replace your value if necessary. This is based on what you want for your family, how you want to provide for them.

I'll tell you frankly: You're not going to be able to get enough life insurance to *fully* replace your entire economic value of your life span.

Insurance companies won't give you that much coverage. There's a table they use. If you're in your 20s, you might get 30 times your income, maybe 20… 15… 10… it depends on your age. Insurers don't want to over-insure someone and then that person either commit suicide or somebody commits foul play. So, you can't just say give me a $10 million policy; you won't get it unless your income and assets justify it.

However, it is important to get the maximum they will allow, so you can get as close as possible to your Human Life Value.

The Different Types of Death and Your Retirement Savings

Dr. Huebner talks about different types of death.

There is actual death—you're in the casket.

There is living death where you're permanently disabled and you have no income coming in. You're still there; the expenses continue, but there's no money to pay those expenses. This is why disability income insurance is so important, especially for a young couple.

Then there is retirement death. When you retire, you're no longer actively producing income from work. You have to rely on your assets to take care of you. Unfortunately, I see so many people go into retirement with no life insurance. So, they have their retirement accounts—401(k)s, 403bs, or profit-sharing plan if they're a business owner.

However, they've got all this money locked up, and they can't enjoy it because they know they have to leave it behind to take care of their spouse in the event of their death.

But if they had life insurance sitting on the side, they could spend more of that retirement money they worked so hard to put away because they know they have life insurance benefits coming in tax free to replace that asset.

CHAPTER 2

How Much Life Insurance Should I Buy?

W HEN IT COMES to life insurance, there are questions that I think everybody should ask. First question is: How much coverage should I have?

To answer that question, let me ask you one first:

If you knew you were going to die tomorrow, and an angel came to your bed tonight and said, "I'm coming back in exactly 24 hours to take you." How much life insurance would you buy?

Most people, when faced with that scenario, answer every dollar they can get. And when you're looking at your whole life especially, that's always the answer—even if you don't know when you're going to die as in the scenario above.

Get as much coverage as the insurance company will give you. If they'll give you $2 million, get $2 million. If you can't afford that much, you could get term insurance in place and upgrade it later. That's called converting, and a bit later in the book, I'll explain why this is such a powerful strategy.

How Much and Why?

If you've gone through the exercise, and you've narrowed down your philosophy to either:

You just want to cover debt, and you've done the needs analysis to figure out how much you need to cover the mortgage, debts, and things like that using your life insurance coverage. Some people just want to leave a clean slate when they die. Nothing wrong with it. This is needs-based planning.

Or you realize you're making a good income today, and you can see where your income is going to go up over the next 15, 20, 30 years that you're working. You want to insure as much as that future growth as you can.

In this case, you've bought into the concept of economic value/ Human Life Value. That means you want to get as much coverage as the life insurance company will allow you to cover your current and future economic. Otherwise the cash value of that future income will be lost forever.

This reminds me of the story of Mr. Kelly—I'll never forget him. He was my very first death benefit claim. I met him 1975 when I had just entered the life insurance business and he was in his late 60s. At first, he didn't want to buy life insurance. He argued with me about it.

Then one day, we were out walking around one of the pastures on his property. And he says, "Okay, son, come to my house tonight and have dinner with us. And we'll clear the table and talk."

So, I'm at his house that night, sat down with his wife and three grown sons. And we ended up getting life insurance for him.

He was charged an extra premium because he was in bad health. He almost didn't take the policy because of that, but we convinced him. His three sons paid the premiums, one-third each. Mr. Kelly had done well financially speaking and had no debt. But the pension he received would die with him. Life insurance was key here.

Thirteen months later, Mr. Kelly died. Because of that life insurance, those adult sons, by paying the premiums, had created tax-free money to take care of Mrs. Kelly until she died. Then what was left over from the investments, we set up went to the sons.

This situation had a very profound impact on me because I was only 23 years old when it happened.

> *"Without that life insurance, she would not have had the income stream she needed."*

Without that life insurance, Mrs. Kelly's income would have been a lot less when her husband died. She would not have had the income stream she needed because her husband's pension would have disappeared.

That's why economic value, the financial contribution of the person, is the key to determining your life insurance needs.

Of course, this all leads to the question: What type of life insurance should you buy to protect your value? You'll find the answer in the next chapter.

Life Insurance Needs and Wants Could Change Over Time

How much life insurance you want could also change as you go through life. I like to have conversations with my clients twice a year to get a financial update to see if we need to make any tweaks in their investments... as well as life insurance.

CHAPTER 3

What Type of Insurance You Should Buy

WHAT IS THE best type of life insurance to buy? People often ask me this question. It's not one-size-fits-all. There's no one policy that is best for everybody.

The real answer is that the best life insurance for you is the one that meets your needs… and this could change over time.

The best policy is the one in place the day you die!

If that means term insurance—great. Whole life—great. If it's a combination of the two, like I did as a young man building a family, that's great too.

But here's the thing…

I can tell you with certainty, in all my years of doing this, I never had a widow or widower ask, "Was this a term policy or whole life?" They were just grateful that they would be taken care of after their loved one's death. They wouldn't lose their home. They could keep the kids in school.

That's a satisfying part of my work you can't put a dollar value on and a great reminder that at the bare minimum you should have some sort of coverage.

Still, the question remains: What type should you get?

There's a lot of debate over which is better—term life insurance or some type of permanent, whether it be whole life or universal life, indexed universal life, or variable life.

After almost half a century of doing this, I've seen so many flavors of the month. It's unbelievable. But life insurance really comes down to two basic types of coverage. And this has been the case since I got into the life insurance business.

Temporary coverage/term life insurance

Permanent coverage/whole life insurance, universal life insurance, variable, or indexed universal life

Let me explain the terms.

Term insurance is like renting or leasing an apartment or a house.

You don't own it; you're leasing it. Now, if I'm the landlord, I get to raise the rents, right? I can raise the rents on you. And at the end of the period, I can kick you out. Say, we had a 20-year term limit on your lease, and I need you to leave now because I'm going to sell the place. Or I have a friend who wants to move in. On the other side, the renter has flexibility. They can pick up and move because they don't have a property tying them down.

Whole life insurance would be like owning a home.

You own whole life coverage; you build up equity. There are tax benefits. Just like home ownership. Many of us want to own our homes because we have control and pride over the ownership. It's the same with whole life insurance.

Term Insurance or Not?

A friend of mine who's my age, 68 years old, has always had term insurance. But now he's realized he's paid these premiums for 20 years, and he didn't die. He's healthy.

So, his term insurance isn't working for him anymore at his age. He needs to convert to whole life coverage. Young couples, on the flipside, should get loaded on all the terms they can get and upgrade it later.

Term Insurance In-Depth

With term life insurance, you have it for a limited period of time. The most common term plan used today is a 20-year level term. Some people do a 30-year term... or 10-year... 15-year... 25-year. But typically, the industry has been promoting 20-year term insurance.

Term insurance is beneficial because it gives us a lot of coverage for a very low premium. So, if a young couple in their 30s is starting out life, and if we buy into the concept of insuring their full economic potential, or Human Life Value, then they're going to need a lot of life insurance.

"It gives us a lot of coverage for a very low premium."

For example, let's suppose that they're each making $100,000 a year, and they've got 30 years to work. 30 times $100,000 is $3 million. So, ideally, we'd want to get $3 million of life insurance on each of them.

Term insurance is very affordable. If they're healthy, it's not going to hurt their financial position. Now, having said that, the likelihood that those term policies are going to result in the death claim is very, very slim. Very few term policies result in a death claim.

I often encounter people who have been paying term premiums all those years, and then they are still living, and they say, "Wait a minute, I paid all that money in premiums. Plus, I lost interest on my premiums. And now I'm losing my insurance because the premium is so high if I try to renew it."

I do see that a lot. So, what would be the reason to pursue this coverage for this young couple?

If I am that young couple, or I'm even single, and I foresee a big future in front of me, I want to protect that future for somebody that I care about, like my spouse, my parents, or even another family member who took care of me and encouraged me and helped me until I got married and had a family. So, I tell people, just because you're single or don't have children, it does not mean that you shouldn't be insured. You should be insured.

And not just to help your loved ones. You should be insured as early as possible, with term insurance if appropriate, because when you need it later, you may not be able to get it due to health issues.

More on this type of conversion later in the book.

Whole Life Insurance In-Depth

This is the type of insurance I prefer to use. There are several different flavors:

- Whole life
- 10-pay policies (designed to be paid up at 10 years)
- 20-pay policies (designed to be paid up at 20 years)
- Paid up at 95 (designed to be paid up when you reach age 95)
- Paid up at 99
- Paid up at 121

Whole life insurance can be a way to force yourself to save money, like taking money out of your paycheck for a 401(k). The first year or two you own a policy, there may be no cash build up, kind of like starting a business. But when you keep the policy and keep putting money in, it becomes a sort of savings plan because it can build cash.

Going back to the owning a home analogy, you build equity when you buy a house. But you don't have any equity initially because the majority of your mortgage payment is going to pay interest, not the principal. So, very little goes to principal, and a lot goes to interest. And then over the years, you'll find that you are making a big dent on the principal.

As far as cash value of the whole life policy, we can design it to be low cash value or high cash value, depending on the desires of the individual.

There are different whole life policies designed for different purposes. It just depends upon the client's situation and what we think we want to happen 10, 15, 20 years down the road.

Putting the Two Together

The variety of different types of term and whole life insurance gives policy owners a huge toolbox.

Often, people use a combination of term and whole life insurance; that's what most of my clients have done over the years.

A solid strategy for first-timers is to take out small whole life policies initially with a lot of term insurance. Later, the term policies are gradually converted to whole life as the policies outlive their usefulness.

In the case of term insurance, people often have a negative view. The scenario is they get to the end of their term, say 20 years, and they feel like they've been paying all this money in premiums, and now that the term is ending, they have nothing to show for it.

Not so.

In fact, what you have is money you've saved or invested during that term.

Now, instead of putting it in the bank, or credit union, or your 401(k), or your mutual fund, you should consider putting at least some of it toward converting your term policy to whole life. If you've set up your term policy to be converted in that way, you're set.

Both term and whole life are important.

I personally no longer have term coverage. I have upgraded my term along the way to where all I have now is permanent, whole life insurance because of the cash values in my policies.

My cash values earn more interest than I get at the bank, higher than bonds, and they never go down. They go up every month. With whole life, you can also reach a point of not paying premiums anymore. So, you have coverage in place without having to pay premiums out of pocket, whereas with term, if you stop, then the company stops insuring you.

Also, the other huge benefit with having whole life policies is that if you choose to, you can use the cash values in many ways. I used my cash values many times over the years to buy a house, buy cars, invest in my business, etc.

Upgrading Your Insurance

I focus on term insurance and whole life. Most people will use a combination of the two although for younger couples and individuals, having all term is fine. The first obligation is to cover yourself as much as possible based on your needs and what you can pay in premiums and then *upgrade it later.*

Let me use my own story to explain why the ability to upgrade—not to mention buying life insurance as early in life as possible—can be so important.

I'll give you two dates here: June 10, 2008, and July 10, 2008.

On June 10, 2008, I filed an application in my office for another $1 million of term life insurance with my company. And because I was on blood pressure medication, I was not allowed to write a check to bind the coverage. They wouldn't take the money. So, we had to send the application to the company for their review first.

During this review, they wrote to my doctors and followed other procedures. Then, July 10, 30 days later, I'm having open heart surgery because a week prior to that, I started having issues. When I went to the doctor, we discovered that I had some blockage in three arteries—one was 10%, another was 90%, and the last was 100%. So, open-heart surgery was needed—a triple bypass!

As you might guess, the insurance company processing my application at that time would not issue the policy after they found out about that procedure. They told me I was uninsurable. However, if I had been able to bind that coverage before surgery, I would have the additional $1 million dollar policy.

That's why it's so important to buy when we're healthy.

"It's so important to buy when we're healthy."

And if cash flow is tight right now, get yourself all the term insurance you can get with a company that offers what we call term conversion opportunities to good old-fashioned dividend paying whole life insurance sometime in the future.

As you can see, there is definitely a place for term insurance too. It does give you the most death benefit for the premium you pay. But just make sure that whatever term you get, you can upgrade to permanent coverage later. Because the day will come when you'll need or want it.

CHAPTER 4

When to Buy Life Insurance... and Who to Buy It From

When should you buy life insurance?
Now!
What are you waiting for?

W E DON'T KNOW when our time is coming or what other issues might pop up when it comes to our health or life situation. That's why securing life insurance as soon as possible is so important.

For one thing, you're more insurable when you are young and pay lower premiums. If you get sick or start suffering from a serious medical condition, you might not be able to get life insurance, or the premiums could be too high.

Like in my case, I had open heart surgery. For a period of time, I could not get new life insurance. Thankfully, I already had a lot of term insurance I had bought previously, which I was able to upgrade—we call that converting to whole life insurance. But, if I didn't have any coverage at all, or very little, I would have been stuck until this day.

My Early Education in the Unexpected

The truth is you never know when you're going to die. Most of us are going to live full to retirement age and beyond. But some will die early.

It gets me thinking of a couple I worked with in 2008. The husband had agreed on life insurance: $3 million term and $3 million whole life policies. He was ready to go but wanted to get to it after he got back from a trip. I urged him not to wait because he had policies approved, and he was very underinsured. He decided to take the coverage before he left.

Good thing, too, as it could have been horrible if not. In August of that year, he died in an accident. Around that time, the stock market was down, real estate was down… everything was crashing during the Great Recession. All his other assets were worth much less.

> *"His insurance policies ensured his wife and kids were taken care of."*

However, his insurance policies ensured his wife and kids were taken care of in this difficult personal and economic period thanks to that money coming in tax free.

Of course, that might not be the case with many families as happened with another one I worked with years ago.

In the early 1980s, a gentleman was in my office late one night; I was working with him until 9 p.m. on putting together his policy. I did everything in the world I could do to get him to give me a check to bind the coverage on the policy right then. But he said he had to sleep on it, that he would let me know tomorrow.

Again, I urged him to leave a check. If he'd left the check there, he'd have been covered from that point on.

"She was devastated emotionally and financially."

Sadly, he lost control of his car and hit a big oak tree on the way home and was killed. His wife called me and said, "Please tell me that my husband gave you a check." He did not, and she was devastated emotionally from the loss of her husband and financially due to the loss of his income.

Over the years, I thought about what I could have done differently to make that man give me a check. But I finally understood that I can't make anyone do anything. I can't hypnotize anyone into giving me their money.

All I can do is provide information and insight—straight talk— in a respectful manner.

You have to make the decision.

Life Insurance and Social Security

If you don't have enough life insurance and little savings, I recommend you delay taking Social Security as long as you can because in this case, that benefit will be vital to your surviving spouse.

You get an 8% increase in your benefit every year you
wait between full retirement age and age 70.

Who to Buy Life Insurance From?

There can be some misunderstandings and misconceptions
about life insurance. Sometimes when I approach people about
coverage, they tell me I'm just trying to sell them a policy and
make a commission.

From my point of view, the money I make from the sale, even
if a person gives me their whole paycheck, it won't change my
lifestyle at all. But if their spouse loses that paycheck because
this person didn't purchase life insurance, they may have to
change their lifestyle.

The point is that I'm a financial advisor. I don't have to sell life
insurance. I'm not under gun point to make a certain quota
each quarter.

I look at the complete financial picture of my clients. We discuss
goals for life and retirement. Then we design a plan to reach
those goals. It's part of my plan, not product philosophy.

That's why you should buy life insurance from a financial
advisor who understands the various options and different life
insurance products… and how to use those products to help you
achieve your financial goals.

As a financial advisor, I prefer to start with the planning first and
then find the product. Sales reps do it the other way around.
And often, due to pressure from management, they will try to

get you to buy certain products, even if they're not a good fit for you.

Another thing you should know about me is that I never give a "hard sale." As I've said, I present the information, my recommendations, and my reasoning—it's up to you to make the decision.

If you've ever worked with an insurance company sales rep, you know the experience can be quite different. I've heard agents say, "Well, If you don't buy this insurance, that just proves you don't love your family."

If someone said that to me, I'd kick them out. That's why I take a more understanding approach. I realize that you might not be able to afford the premiums right now for all the coverage you really need. But I will work to get you as much coverage as possible, using all the strategies I know.

Forget the Online Apps and 800 Numbers

You do have many options for where to buy life insurance.

You can buy life insurance online. You don't need to meet with an agent; you can get online and buy life insurance. But do you want to deal with an 800 number? Or do you want to deal with a loving, caring professional who's there with you and can help you?

Someone who understands all the different types of insurance and how to use them. It's not just life insurance; it's how it coordinates with disability insurance if you're still working.

Plus, you need to predict the loss of future income and calculate total Human Life Value. And, if that wasn't enough, you also have to contend with your changing life insurance needs over the years.

Yes, you can go online to buy life insurance in minutes. But I'll tell you, you'll probably get stuck when you see the options and don't understand which of those tools will work for you. Good luck getting the level of help you really need with an app or salesperson.

My recommendation is to work with a professional who understands life insurance, all the things it can be used for, and how it fits into your overall financial plan.

It's sort of like going into a hardware store and browsing the tools. Unless you're very handy, there are probably several you're not familiar with—you don't know what they do. Or you might have a project in mind... but you don't know which of those tools is needed for the job.

That's the value of talking to someone you can trust to advise you on the type of insurance to get and how it will fit into your full financial picture. This is the best way to get insurance coverage that will fit your purposes.

Thinking of Canceling Your Life Insurance? Read This First

I get really angry when some knucklehead advises someone to cancel their life insurance because they don't need it.

If you've been advised to do so or are considering it for some other reason, call your insurance company first and ask this question:

Are my dividends enough to pay the premiums?

If not, you can ask to switch to a reduced paid-up policy where you'll make no more payments but still get some coverage. You don't want to leave yourself with no life insurance at all.

CHAPTER 5

How to Use Life Insurance the Right Way, Even Before You Die

M ANY PEOPLE THINK that life insurance is all about the death benefit. This money goes to your family when you die—that's it.

Wrong!

At this point in the book, you've no doubt realized that there's a whole lot more to life insurance than you've ever been told. In this chapter, you'll discover that you can use your coverage in many ways. It's much more than the death benefit.

We'll explore how you can get the most value from your life insurance program.

Part of the problem is that it's misnamed. You know what it should be called? Success insurance. I can't call it that. Regulators wouldn't like it.

> *"You can actually benefit from life insurance without having to die."*

But the truth is that life insurance is a tool that can be used to great benefit at different stages during your life. It can play a role in the lives of somebody in their early 20s, a grandchild, a young couple, business owners, retirees... everybody.

My mindset is that life insurance is nothing more than a powerful financial tool... that's useless if you never use it.

First, you should understand that if you have life insurance, properly designed, you'll feel good knowing that your family is taken care of when you die. Yes, that's the death benefit.

Therefore, you can do other things with your money. You can be more aggressive with your investments. You can take more risks—you could get involved in real estate, for example. In other words, you could pursue other avenues to potential financial returns.

Without life insurance, you have to play it safe because you don't have that guaranteed income for your family the policy would bring.

Going Beyond the Death Benefit

You should think of life insurance as a tool you can use in many ways to achieve certain goals. Think of it like a saw. You could use it to cut baseboards and trim in your home or cut two-by-fours for a playhouse out back for the kids.

"It's all about accessing the cash values in your policies."

It could be used to eliminate debt... cover college expenses... pay taxes... fund a business... bring you more income in retirement, if need be.

It's all about accessing the cash values in your policies. That's your money building up, and you are allowed to use it.

I remember one of my doctor clients coming in one time. He looked white as a sheet, and I asked, "What's wrong, Doc?" He said, "I can't meet payroll for my office staff. And I have to tell 12 people I can't pay them."

It turns out he didn't have any money because he had made a bad investment. So, I brought up the cash value on his life insurance policy. He had $350,000 right there. We called his banker. I explained that he had $350,000 in cash value, and I was going to send him over to see the banker with a collateral assignment form. He only needed $75,000 to cover payroll. He got that money from the bank. The banker accepted the policy and the cash value as collateral for a loan.

My Own Journey – and How You Can Learn From My Experiences

Before I reveal other strategies for using life insurance, I'd like to share a personal story that illustrates how I got into this industry... how it has changed over the years... and how I've adapted to those changes both professionally and personally.

I bought my first life insurance policy when I was in the Air Force. I was ordered to go to a presentation and bought a $10,000 policy. When I got out of the service and moved to Tallahassee in 1974, my plan was to go to law school at Florida State. But I ended up pursuing another career due to a chance meeting.

I bumped into a friend one day and went to breakfast, and he convinced me to buy a life insurance policy. It was a $25,000 whole life policy. But he also encouraged me to look into getting into the business for myself.

That's how my career began.

Back in 1975, all we did was life insurance. No investments. No planning. Everybody stayed in their lane back then. The mutual fund salesman did his thing. The stockbroker did his thing. The banker did his thing. And the life insurance guy did his thing.

Then the financial industry changed, and everybody was forced to become a jack of all trades.

That's when I quickly realized that for me to have a long-term, sustainable business, I couldn't just sell life insurance. So, I branched into advising people on their financial and retirement planning. I look at the whole financial picture. And a big part of that is still life insurance.

In fact, I think life insurance is probably the most important thing we do.

When I first got into the insurance business, most of the clients were young and single.

I just told them my story, explaining why I owned life insurance as a young man and how it worked.

I had options, called riders, that would allow me to increase my coverage later, even if I were unhealthy. We call those future insurability options, sometimes called GIOs or guaranteed insurability options.

Along the way, I just kept acquiring coverage. And then when I got married, it became obvious that I had bigger responsibilities, bigger obligations, so I increased my coverage. And then I looked at everything, just like I advise my clients, and I felt like I wanted a large amount of life insurance to cover debt, the mortgage, car payments...

I wanted to make sure, in the event of my death, that my wife could stay home and raise our son and not have to go to work. So, I bought life insurance to guarantee that.

Fortunately, I didn't die. I'm still here. But I am still able to benefit after paying for policies all those years.

The life insurance that I bought early on was mostly term insurance because I could get a lot of protection for a very low cost.

By having the life insurance in place, I was able to be in a position where I could save money, invest money, and put money into my 401(k). And I was able to make business decisions because I knew that if something did happen to me, whether I died or became disabled, that income would come in to take care of my young family.

I think back to May 1994 when we were buying a house. My plan was to use some of the money in my mutual funds for the down payment and closing costs. Well, the market was down. So, I said, "Well, if I take it out of there, we will have a permanent loss." Instead, I did a policy loan on my life insurance policy, paid the closing costs and the down payment. And then when the market went back up, I cashed in some of the mutual funds to pay back my life insurance loan.

Not only did I buy my house using life insurance, but I've also bought a rental property and a little place on the Florida River. I've even bought equipment using policies to get a direct loan from the insurance company.

And let me clarify what that means because people often say you're just borrowing your own money. But that's not accurate.

Accessing the Cash Values of Your Life Insurance

When I borrowed money from the insurance company, they used my cash value as collateral. So think in terms of a bank. Let's say I've got $20,000 at the bank, and I need $20,000 to make a purchase. I can either go cash in my $20,000 and not have a loan, or I can say I've got $20,000 sitting here, how about loaning me $20,000 and use the cash in my bank account as collateral.

In that way, my money is still in the bank, earning interest and growing, while I'm using their money until I pay it back.

> *"When you borrow against your policy, you're borrowing the company's money."*

Life insurance can work in the same way. When you borrow against your policy, you're borrowing the company's money.

Years ago, I made a sizable business purchase: a big projector for presentations that hooked up to my computer. When those first came out, they were expensive. I borrowed from a life insurance policy to buy one.

Why use the insurance? Because the interest rate was lower than doing it through the bank at the time or financing it with the people who were selling the machine.

I'm not the only one. If you look back at the lives of some very famous people, you can see how they used life insurance in similar ways.

Business Benefits with Life Insurance
Brothers Walt and Roy Disney had reached a point in the construction of Disneyland where the banks would not lend them any more money. So, they used the cash value in their life insurance policies.

JCPenney founder James Cash Penney, who grew one store into a whole chain of dozens of stores across the Rocky Mountain states, was devastated by the stock market crash of 1929. The impact of the Great Depression forced him to borrow against his life insurance to meet employee payroll. If not for that loan, this department store, which was very influential in the retail industry, might not have survived.

These are just a couple examples of using the cash value in your life insurance policy when the banks won't work with you.

This strategy, as you see in the case of JCPenney, is especially effective in times of economic crisis.

Using Life Insurance in Times of Crisis

Think back to the Great Financial Crisis of 2008 and 2009. Back then, I had good friends who had gotten overextended in real estate. We had to use their cash value in life insurance policies to bail them out, so the bank wouldn't foreclose on them.

My mother used this strategy too. She wanted to buy a car years ago. The interest rate back then was 12% for this car loan. I told her it was way too high, and the monthly payments were pretty high too.

Using a loan against the cash value in her life insurance allowed her to pay what she wanted to pay—$100 instead of the $200 the bank wanted for the car loan. She paid it back on schedule, and I put the money back into her policy. At one point, I just paid off the balance on her behalf.

In another case, I worked with a young couple building a home. They had reached a point where the bank wouldn't give them any more money. The construction was being delayed, and they didn't know what to do.

They needed about $11,000. I told them they had a lot more than that in their life insurance cash values. So, we called the bank and had a conversation. The banker agreed to use that cash value as collateral for a loan, and the couple finished their house.

The couple had a dinner party and said in front of everyone: "This house may not have happened without John Curry's influence."

All these stories show the wide range of ways you can use the case value in your life insurance policies.

Life Insurance as an "Asset Class"

In many ways, whole life insurance is nothing more than saving money. It has many other benefits compared to traditional retirement accounts when you start stripping away all the layers of the onion and understanding it.

When Roth IRAs came out, I laughed my tail off because everybody thought it was the greatest thing. But here's something to consider.

You put $5,000 in a Roth IRA, and then you die. What does your family get? Maybe $5,000. But what if the stock market was down 20%? Now, they only get $4,000. If the market is up 20%, maybe they get $6,000.

But if you put that $5,000 in a life insurance policy, and you die, they may get more than $5,000. Tax free. If you become disabled, who's going to fund your Roth IRA? Nobody. But if you qualify for the waiver of premium[1] feature, the life insurance payments are waived on your behalf. That means you don't pay premiums while you qualify for the benefit.

---

[1] A Waiver of Premium rider waives the obligation for the policyholder to pay further premiums should he or she become totally disabled continuously for at least six months. This rider will incur an additional cost. See policy contract for additional details and requirements.

CHAPTER 6

Life Insurance Works in Every Stage of Life

I'VE HAD PEOPLE say, "I'm single. I don't need life insurance." But as mentioned before, everyone has an economic value. If I can get to someone in their 20s and get them to understand the value of insuring their future, they're so much better off.

For young couples, especially just starting out in life, they have a plan to buy a home, possibly have a family. But what if one of them gets sick? Do they have a plan for this possibility?

What about kids?

In June 2012, I was at a convention in California. I got a call in the wee hours from my wife. Our son had been in a terrible accident, and deputies had to come to the house to let her know he was undergoing brain surgery.

Our son is doing well now. But for a number of years, he was not able to work. Life insurance stepped in.

Because of something called a waiver of premiums, his policies were paid by the insurance company. I didn't have to pay anything. I could put that money toward his care. When he was healthy and back at work, I started paying the premiums again.

I just bought new life insurance for my son, who's now 37. Yes, he sustained those injuries during his car accident. Fortunately, when he was a kid, seven years old, I purchased life insurance on him with future insurability options. So, I'm still able to acquire insurance for him. I own it. All the cash build-up is my asset. I'm just saving money.

"If something happens to him, money will come in tax free."

But if something happens to him, money will come in tax free that will allow me to take care of his son, my grandson. I also have life insurance on my grandson for the same reasons.

I will say right now, unequivocally, every young couple I get in front of, I tell them get all the coverage you can right now. Don't worry about anything except getting term insurance that we can upgrade later for you.

And for all the folks my age (68), if you've got excess money in savings, and you know you're not going to use it, what better way to help your adult children and grandchildren kickstart their futures by using insurance.

Now, let's take an in-depth look at the many ways you can use your life insurance at different stages of life. Some will not apply to you personally. However, it may apply to your family members, and I would suggest you talk to them about these concepts and encourage them to learn about it themselves.

Single

When you're single, some people say categorically you don't need life insurance. You may not need it. But it's very possible you might. Because remember, life insurance should be based on your Human Life Value, your economic value.

And no matter who you are, you have an economic value. And people without a family should consider owning life insurance.

For a young, single person, let's say in their 20s, the reason to have life insurance is to protect their future.

At this point in life, you probably don't even know what you're going to do for a career yet; you might even be in college. When I first started in the life insurance business, a lot of my clients were college students at Florida State University, Florida A&M, and Tallahassee Community College. They would buy a life insurance policy to help them save money and protect their future.

If you're a young person concerned about your future because you plan on going to law school, medical school, or whatever… why wouldn't you consider getting a large term life insurance policy at a low cost? Then, if you have health issues later, you already have your coverage in place. Or perhaps you do a combination of a large amount of term and a smaller portion of whole life that has guaranteed insurability options.

That's what I did for my grandchildren. So, they have the guarantee they can buy more insurance in the future, even if they have poor health.

"At this stage, it's really about locking it in at a low cost during the years where you're at your peak health."

You see, at this stage, it's really about locking it in at a low cost during the years where you're at your peak health, so that as you get older, the cost doesn't change.

The most precious asset you have is your health. Think of it this way: You pay for life insurance with money called premiums. But you really buy it with your good health because if you're not healthy, no matter how much money you've got, you can't get it.

There are people I know who would love to get life insurance, and they have money sitting in investments and retirement accounts. But they can't get insurance because they're uninsurable.

So, to me, the most precious thing is to use your good health. Lock that coverage in today, and the insurance company must honor that in the future as long as you keep paying premiums.

This happened to me with my open-heart surgery. On my term insurance policies, they had to give me a preferred rating when I upgraded to whole life, even though I had heart surgery, because it's a contractual obligation.

Young Couple

With a young couple, it's also important to lock in coverage early in life, just as with single people. Both spouses should do it.

Life insurance covers the financial future in the case of an untimely death.

That's why I tell young couples to get as much term insurance as they can to lock in coverage. And if they are able to save money, I recommend that they start their life insurance portfolio and add some whole life coverage as well as disability insurance coverage. Because if either one of them can't work, they need money coming to cover the mortgage, car payments, and other expenses.

Young Family

Again, make sure you get as much coverage as possible. Here an untimely death will have an even more devastating impact on the spouse and the kids as well because you're leaving behind a spouse who has to take care of the children by themselves. And you know how hard raising kids is with the two of you.

The surviving spouse in these cases loses their partner in life, an emotional blow, as well as their economic value. Life insurance provides the income they need to keep going and maintain their lifestyle.

Soon to Retire

For the purposes of this book, I define soon to retire as someone 10 to 15 years out from retirement—someone about 50 or so, whose kids have moved out, and they're starting to think seriously about retirement.

If they're eligible for a pension, they start thinking about what plan to choose. They look at their Social Security and when to start taking it. Those are things I talk about with my clients.

Life insurance is always part of the plan.

For people at this stage, life insurance becomes important because they had group insurance and it was getting expensive, or they were losing it when they retired. Many people don't give it much thought. They just assume that when they retire, they'll still have their life insurance in place that the employer is providing. And that rarely happens. They lose it. And all of a sudden, they go, "Oh, man, I've got health problems now; can I get coverage?" It's too late then.

So again, secure and lock in your life insurance coverage early in life.

> *"There are several ways soon-to-be retired people can use their life insurance."*

But if you do have it, there are ways soon-to-be retired people can use their coverage.

I have a client I'm working with who's 57. He's in a situation where he wants to help his son, who has a great business opportunity but no money, as is the case with many young people. He might get a loan from the bank because interest rates are so low. But I also showed him that, if necessary, he has enough from his investment money and life insurance cash values to give the money his son needs.

What we're really talking about is going to the bank and saying, I have this cash value over here in my life insurance policy that over the years I've saved by paying the premiums that contribute to the cash value. And it's effectively a pile of money. And I'm willing to put that up as collateral, if you'll loan me the money that I need for this opportunity.

I have a line of credit on two of my life insurance policies. I could borrow directly from the insurance company or with today's low interest rates, I could use the bank's money.

I did tell my client that either way, he should buy life insurance on his son to protect his investment.

Why take a loan and not just cash out that money from your policy?

If you cashed it in, you just lost your death benefit and you just lost the power of compounding. So, instead of me taking money out of my policy, I'm better off leaving it alone, going over to the bank, and using their money or borrowing from the insurance company instead of cashing it in.

Leaving Money to Charity

I have two policies on me that are payable to foundations in the event of my death because I want the work that they're doing to continue. And obviously, in the event of my death, the money I'm contributing now would die with me. By having the life insurance policies in place, and those foundations as beneficiaries, they will have money that they can invest and use the earnings to continue the work that I believe in.

Business Owners

If you own a business or are thinking about owning a business, there are ways life insurance can be useful to you.

Here's an actual case with one of my clients who was a business owner. He had a bank loan to run his business, and he also had a mortgage on his building.

While we were talking during a review, I asked him, "Why don't you get a key person life insurance policy on yourself, so that the business would receive this money to pay off the business debt. Then let's have a personal life insurance policy that you own, so that in the event of your death, your wife could pay the mortgage off on the building and have that building as an asset that she could rent."

This conversation took place in the 1980s. In 1992, he died of a heart attack. By having those policies, both business and personal, that were structured properly, his widow was able to keep the building and keep key employees to run the business until she was ready to sell it later.

How to Use Life Insurance for Your Children and Grandchildren

I bought a $125,000 life insurance policy on my grandson. I did it because there are eight future insurability options that he can exercise starting at age 25, and every three years thereafter until he's had those eight options.

This guarantees my grandson can get an additional $2 million of life insurance no matter his health.

I know that I have protected his future insurability.

I did the same thing when my son was seven. And because of an automobile accident he had, I have been exercising those options on his policy every three years. So, I've been acquiring more insurance on him even though he probably would not qualify if starting fresh.

Again, here you can see why it's so important to get your life insurance early. You lock in coverage for the rest of your life, even if you have poor health or become otherwise uninsurable later.

Admittedly, it's hard to think about buying life insurance for your kids. It's uncomfortable thinking about your child dying. But if one of your children died, what type of condition do you think you're going to be in? Emotionally, you're going to be screwed up, probably unable to work. So there's going to be some financial issues.

"I've encouraged clients to insure their children and grandchildren."

That's why from early in my career, I've encouraged clients to insure their children and grandchildren.

Important: You should own it, control it, and not give it to them. As long as I'm living, I will own and pay the premiums on the policies I have on my children, grandchildren, and great-grandchildren. This way, I know that if something happens to my son or daughter, I will have money coming in tax free to take care of my grandkids and even my great grandkids.

By paying those premiums, I'm saving money that I can use later if I need it.

After my death, those policies will transfer to the insured person. They can either continue the policies or cash them in and destroy the plan I set up for them. The choice is theirs. But they have a plan that will help them in retirement if they choose to use it. Because if they don't do anything else in life, the money that's in there now will continue to grow to provide them some retirement income.

Does Buying Life Insurance for the Wife and Kids Make You Squeamish?

I own life insurance not only on myself, but also my children and grandchildren.

People may tell you that you don't need life insurance on kids, that you don't need life insurance on your spouse.

Potential clients have told me that they don't want to profit if something happens to their spouse or kids. Here's the thing: Buying life insurance doesn't mean they're going to die prematurely, and you can't think of it as profiting from their death.

Probably nothing will happen to them. That's the nature of insurance. But if something did happen, you might be unable to work because of emotional issues, or some other issue could pop up related to the loss, and the life insurance will be invaluable then.

A client years ago would not let me insure his wife. He said they didn't need it because she wasn't working or bringing in an income.

Well, she died of a massive heart attack. Economically, she was worth a lot because he didn't take into account all the work she did to take care of him and their three children. He ended up having to hire a full-time nanny to help. Life insurance would have helped with those significant expenses.

CHAPTER 7

How to Use Life Insurance in Retirement

I N GENERAL, THERE are four ways your income stops:
You lose your job.
You become disabled and can't work because of health issues.
Death.

Those are involuntary income losses. Then there is...

Retirement.

Yes, retirement! That's when one day, instead of going to work and earning a paycheck, you decide to use the assets you've accumulated, Social Security, and/or a pension to fund your life.

People have been told that when they retire, they don't need their life insurance anymore. So, they cancel it. That's a big mistake because they lose that protection, safety, and growing cash value, not to mention the death benefit for their survivors.

At retirement, life insurance is just as important, if not more so, than at any other period in your life.

The simple fact is that people who retire with large amounts of life insurance, especially whole life, have a more secure retirement than people who retire with no life insurance.

Why?

Because your life insurance cash values never have a bad day. No matter what's going on in the market, those cash values go up every day, unlike traditional retirement accounts, mutual funds, and stocks. You get guaranteed cash value. Granted, the dividend part could go up or down each year. But once it's posted to your account, it can never be taken away from you as long as premiums are paid on the policy remains inforce.

This makes life insurance an ideal retirement savings account, one that you can tap into, if need be, that's not impacted by the ups and downs in the market. It's a great way to diversify your nest egg.

But that's just the beginning...

Using Life Insurance as Part of Your Overall Retirement Strategy

If you have the ability to save money, you should be putting some of it, in my opinion, toward permanent, whole life insurance.

Right now, with the amount of cash I have in my policies, if I chose to, I could turn that cash into a guaranteed stream of income for the rest of my life. So, in effect, I could create my own pension if I wanted to give up some or all of the death benefit.

In my case, on paper, I'm retired. I'm collecting Social Security and pensions, but I'm still working. And I'm still putting money in my life insurance policies. I just paid two premiums two weeks ago, as a matter of fact.

Why?

Because when I put the money in, my cash values increase, and that money is protected from lawsuits and creditors in the state of Florida. Plus, I'm not paying any tax on the gain until I take it out… and my death benefit increases each year.

I don't have to pay premiums anymore because the policies are self-sufficient—the dividends could pay the premiums. But I'm still putting money in because I like the terms a lot better than the interest in a bank account or the risk of the stock market.

And that's only the beginning of what your whole life insurance could do.

"Cash values are protected from lawsuits and creditors."

I also can use it as collateral to borrow money from the bank, or I can use it to do a policy loan from the company. There are a lot of things I can do with that money. And I will tell you this, I love the fact that my cash values are protected from lawsuits and creditors. This is the case in most states. In Florida, we have unlimited protection.

With whole life, you don't pay tax on the cash values as they grow. When you take the money out, if you have a taxable gain, you'll have some taxes on that. But, if you take it out properly, you won't have to pay any tax.

Life Insurance as a Backstop

Life insurance can also give you the freedom to spend down your current assets.

Let me give you two examples:

For people who are in pension plans, which are rare these days unless you work for the government:

I'll use the Florida Retirement System as an example. You have four options. You can take option one, which gives you the most income, but upon your death, the income dies with you. Or option two, which gives you a lifetime income that is only guaranteed to the beneficiary for 10 years. So, if you die after 10 years, there is no more money. Or you can take option three, which is joint with 100%. This means whatever you were getting will continue to go to your spouse, but it's less money than you could have gotten with option one or two. The fourth option is whatever you were getting, the spouse would get two-thirds of it. If your spouse dies first, you also will get only two-thirds.

I had to make these choices. I wanted to make sure I had enough life insurance in place, so that when I retired, I could take the higher pension.

I did that. I took a pension option that is _life_ to me and a guaranteed 10 years. I'm two years into that pension. If I live 10 years and die, that pension would die with me. But my life insurance comes in to replace that for the people that I want to get the money.

Another example is with Social Security. I had a recent case with clients that illustrates this. I'll make up the numbers to keep the math simple. His Social Security benefits are $2,000 a month. His wife gets $1,000. In the event of his death, she's going to get the higher number. But that's still a $1,000 loss, isn't it?

How can you replace that? I showed this client he had already solved that problem because he had life insurance in place. That policy can replace the income lost from Social Security.

Why Does the Government Like Life Insurance?

The reason that life insurance enjoys such a tax favored status in our tax code is because it provides a social good. When I was getting my master's degree in financial services, we spent a lot of time on understanding tax policy, tax issues, and life insurance and annuities, and IRAs and 401(k)s. A reason they get granted tax-favored status is because it's encouraging us to do something that needs to be done—putting away money.

Because if we did not do them, the government would have even more fiscal problems. If there were no life insurance, can you imagine the number of people who would need assistance from the government?

Using Life Insurance to Avoid the Deferred Tax Trap

Another example I see all the time is people who have been very frugal and have saved a lot of money. They've got $300,000... $400,000 in their state deferred comp, 403(b) plan, or their 401(k) or IRA. But they've forgotten about the tax burden. And they say, "Well, I'm going to leave this money to my children."

The plan is to take it as a lump sum. That triggers tax law provisions.

If you leave money to a non-spouse beneficiary, they have to take the money out over a 10-year period or as a lump sum. In either case, by year 10, that money has to be withdrawn with an inherited IRA. And I won't go any further because I don't want to get too complicated talking about taxes. But the short story is that tax will be paid on that money at some point. When you take it out and enjoy the income or when your family gets it after your death, they get less of it because of these taxes.

But there is another way.

You can "pre-pay the tax," if you will.

You could take a chunk of the money, whether it be from retirement assets, another asset, or out of cash flow, and use it to pay life insurance premiums. That way the tax gets paid, and the life insurance flows in tax free to replace the tax that was paid.

Are You Relying on Group Life Insurance from Work?

I often see clients who are retired or very close to it, and they haven't given a thought to the fact that when they stop working, they lose their group life insurance. One lady has $87,000 in a group policy, and she had planned to give it to her daughter when she died. Unfortunately, with that type of insurance the coverage ended at her retirement.

Now, this lady wanted to buy life insurance on her own to ensure her daughter's future. Because she's older, her premiums are more expensive than if she had bought in her 40s. So, she's having to cut back the savings she puts into her credit union and put it towards life insurance.

Conclusion

I N THIS BOOK, we started off talking about your most valuable asset, your Human Life Value, also referred to as your economic value.

We've talked about how much life insurance you should buy.

We've talked about the different types and which ones you should buy... when you should buy it... who you should buy it from... and how to use it in various situations throughout life, including in retirement.

Throughout my 46-year career, I've helped people use this tool we call life insurance in every phase of life.

Young, older, married, single, with kids, business owner, professional executive... doesn't matter where you are in life, there are many ways to use different financial tools with this coverage.

"It comes down to planning and strategy."

But, you have to know these tools are available and how to use them properly. It comes down to planning and strategy, keeping in mind the regulations, tax rules, and other factors, as well as coordinating with the other pieces of your financial life, like retirement accounts, investments, and savings.

When the time comes for us to die, it's not just how much money you had, but how much you got to keep. How much you passed on… your legacy.

You should want life insurance even if you think you don't need it because of how it protects your life <u>and</u> other financial assets.

Keep in mind that some people that were very successful with real estate investments got hurt bigtime in 2008 and 2009. Those with good investment portfolios also got hurt as the market was down.

If you were to die during a crisis like this, at a time when all this financial calamity is going on, your family could discover that the assets you all were depending on have now become liabilities.

So, I tell people at a minimum, if you're not interested in insuring your Human Life Value (i.e. your current and future economic value), please make sure you have enough to cover all your debt and to cover unexpected expenses and taxes—they always pop up.

Where to Go from Here

There is no magic bullet. But if you can have only one financial product, I would say make it whole life insurance.

There is a lot of debate out there when it comes to life insurance over whether to buy term insurance and invest the difference or buy some type of permanent, whole life coverage. And yes, in some cases, as I've stated, it's a good idea to start with term that you can then convert to whole life later.

But that's not where you should start. The first place to start is with your most valuable asset—that's you.

Your future economic value.

You earn a paycheck today, and hopefully, you'll get pay increases over time. So let's just pretend that you make $100,000 a year, and you have 30 years to work. That's an economic value of $3 million if you never got a pay raise. And of course, you get pay increases along the way. So, it's even higher.

But very few people would look at that and say, okay, so I want to make sure I'll protect that $3 million dollars and get $3 million of life insurance. We don't think that way.

But when it comes to property value, if your home were worth $3 million, you would want to get it insured for replacement value. Because if it got destroyed by fire or hurricane, you'd want it to be replaced. And I just find that it's interesting that we human beings will think that way. And I think sometimes it's because the financial institutions don't take the time to educate us properly.

My Approach

When I work with clients, I give the best thinking I have. I take the approach of a good family physician.

I go to my family doctor, the doctor listens, asks what's happening, what's going on, I explain it, and then, to the best of his ability, he makes a diagnosis, he writes a prescription, and it's up to me to fill the prescription or not.

As I said at the beginning of this book, I believe in straight talk. No graphs. No jargon. I just explain the good, the bad, the ugly.

I don't see or feel the need to beat you over the head with a bunch of printouts and graphs about how great life insurance is. I'll explain conceptually first then demonstrate how it works with a printout. And from there, you can decide which way you want to go.

But we're not going to look at any printouts until we first determine what is your economic value? Do you want to insure that economic value? And what is your financial ability to do so?

Then, we'll start making some decisions.

I'm not trying to convince you that life insurance is the greatest thing. I'm simply saying let's look at your situation and decide what's important to you. Depending on what's important, life insurance could be a tool you should consider using.

It's a personal choice.

If you're ready to explore those choices and see how life insurance might fit into your overall financial, retirement, and estate planning, I'd be happy to speak with you.

> To get started, call the office at 850-562-3000 and one of my team members will help you schedule a 20-minute introductory call.

Additional Resources

The Secure Retirement Podcast

Listen as John discusses key issues for anyone nearing or in retirement and interviews retirees who are living their Secure Retirement.

johnhcurry.com/podcast

Regular Webinars on Important Retirement Topics

Join John and his team for monthly webinars on a range of topics including: The Florida Retirement System, Social Security, Medicare, The 7 Mistakes Most People Make When Planning for a Secure Retirement, and more.

johnhcurry.com/webinar

The Secure Retirement Scorecard

Take the Secure Retirement Scorecard and see where you stand in 10 the key areas. In less than 5 minutes you'll have a sense of where you stand now, and which issues are most important to address next. The scorecard may be found on Page 8 of this book, or you may download a printable copy online.

johnhcurry.com/scorecard

Are you a Member of the Florida Retirement System? Register for our Retirement Planning Course Exclusively for Members of The Florida Retirement System

Here's what you'll discover in this complimentary course:

- FRS Pension Options - What are the four options and how do they work?
- Retirement Accounts - Your options for your 457 Deferred Compensation plans, DROP, 403(b), IRAs and other retirement accounts.
- Social Security - All your Social Security questions answered (plus the ones you didn't even know to ask).
- Medicare - How to navigate the complex topic of Medicare.
- Required Minimum Distributions - What are RMDs? How will they impact your retirement?

info.johnhcurry.com/frs-course

About the Author

J OHN CURRY'S PASSION for helping Members of the FRS plan for their Secure Retirement began with his grandfather and father. Both worked their entire careers at the Florida Department of Transportation and retired under the State of Florida Retirement System. John watched as both men failed to get the guidance they needed, and suffered financial consequences in retirement. John Curry has been on a personal mission to share the wisdom and experience he's gained helping thousands of people from all walks of life prepare for a Secure Retirement with his personal client consultations, books, podcast, DVDs, CDs, seminars, and speeches.

Dear Friend,

Thank you for sharing your time with me as you read this book.
I am a passionate advocate of protecting families and their futures
through what I do. That's why I am writing this note inviting you to
come in for a No cost, No Obligation FOCUS Session.
In the FOCUS Session we will talk about:

Your Future
Your Opportunities
Your Concerns
Your Uniqueness
Your Strengths

At the end of our 45-minute session we will both know if it makes
sense for us to meet again. If yes, we'll schedule another appointment.
If no, we'll part having had the benefit of clarifying your goals and
future. A win for everyone, with NO RISK to you!

John

P.S. This session can also be conducted by phone/computer
conference.